ELEMENTS OF
LIFE

SULFUR

NANCY DICKMANN

PowerKiDS
press

Published in 2019 by **The Rosen Publishing Group, Inc.**
29 East 21st Street, New York, NY 10010

Cataloging-in-Publication Data
Names: Dickmann, Nancy.
Title: Sulfur / Nancy Dickmann.
Description: New York : PowerKids Press, 2019. | Series: Elements of life | Includes glossary and index.
Identifiers: ISBN 9781538347775 (pbk.) | ISBN 9781538347799 (library bound) | ISBN 9781538347782 (6pack)
Subjects: LCSH: Sulfur--Juvenile literature. | Periodic table of the elements--Juvenile literature.
Classification: LCC QD181.S1 D53 2019 | DDC 546'.723--dc23

For Brown Bear Books Ltd:
Text and Editor: Nancy Dickmann
Designer and Illustrator: Supriya Sahai
Design Manager: Keith Davis
Picture Manager: Sophie Mortimer
Editorial Director: Lindsey Lowe
Children's Publisher: Anne O'Daly

Concept development: Square and Circus/Brown Bear Books Ltd

Picture Credits
Front Cover: Artwork, Supriya Sahai.
Interior: Alamy: FLHC 26, 17r; iStock: Terry J Alcorn, 20, asiseeit, 21, Jacques van Deteren, 22–23, fotografiche, 16–17, golero, 24, helovi, 7tr, Leeuwtje, 5, Olga Miltsova, 19, Alexander Moroz, 25br, 29b, nirat, 25t, RM Nunes, 6–7, 28, Peopleimages, 12, Olaf Schmitz, 23, Tomazi, 14, Undefined, 10br; NARA: 17tl; NOAA: Okeanos, 15; Shutterstock: Radek Borovka, 11b, Eric Isselee, 19br, People Image Studio, 9, Norbert Zsolt, 11t, 29t.
Key: t=top, b=bottom, c=center, l=left, r=right

Brown Bear Books have made every attempt to contact the copyright holders. If you have any information please contact licensing@brownbearbooks.co.uk

Manufactured in the United States of America

CPSIA Compliance Information: Batch CWPK19: For Further Information contact Rosen Publishing, New York, New York at 1-800-237-9932

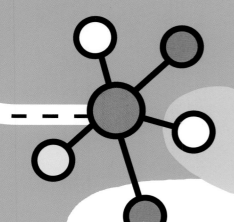

CONTENTS

ELEMENTS ALL AROUND US 4

PHYSICAL PROPERTIES OF SULFUR 6

CHEMICAL PROPERTIES OF SULFUR 8

WHERE IS SULFUR FOUND? 10

SULFUR IN THE BODY 12

SULFUR AND LIFE 14

SULFUR AND MEDICINE 16

SMELLY SULFUR 18

SULFURIC ACID 20

ACID RAIN 22

USING SULFUR 24

The Periodic Table 26

Quiz 28

Glossary 30

Further Resources 31

Index 32

ELEMENTS ALL AROUND US

What do gold, calcium, and oxygen have in common? They are all elements! Elements cannot be broken down into other substances. All living things are made of elements. Oxygen, carbon, hydrogen, nitrogen, phosphorus, and sulfur are the most important to life.

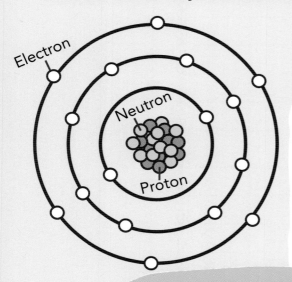

Electron

Neutron

Proton

BREAK IT DOWN

The building block of an element is a tiny unit called an atom. Atoms are much too small to see. They are made of even smaller particles, called protons, neutrons, and electrons. Protons and neutrons are inside the nucleus—the central part of an atom.

THE SULFUR ATOM

A sulfur atom has 16 electrons and 16 protons. Most have 16 neutrons, but a few have more.

SUPER SULFUR

There is sulfur in every living thing. It is also found in rocks and minerals, especially around volcanoes. There is even sulfur in oil and natural gas. Sulfur can often be found in its pure form. Sulfur atoms can also combine with atoms of other elements to form compounds.

Pure sulfur is a solid. It can combine with other elements to make compounds that can be solids, liquids, or gases.

Natural or Not?

There are about 94 elements that are found in nature. Others have been made in laboratories.

PHYSICAL PROPERTIES OF SULFUR

Each element has different properties. Some properties are physical. They can be observed and described without changing the element into another substance.

DIFFERENT FORMS

Sulfur can come in different forms, called allotropes. Each allotrope is pure sulfur, but the atoms are arranged in different patterns. The different arrangements give the allotropes different physical properties.

Sulfur melts to a yellow liquid that gets browner and stickier as the temperature goes up.

LOOKING AT SULFUR

Some of sulfur's physical properties are easy to see, just by using your senses. Its color and odor are both physical properties. Hardness, shininess, and the temperature at which it melts or turns into a gas are physical properties, too.

HARDNESS: Sulfur is not very hard. It is fairly brittle, meaning that it breaks apart easily.

COLOR: Pure sulfur is pale yellow. When melted it can turn reddish-brown if the temperature is high enough.

ODOR: Pure sulfur has no taste or smell, although many sulfur compounds are very smelly.

STRUCTURE: Many allotropes of sulfur form crystals in regular patterns.

CONDUCTIVITY: Sulfur is not a good conductor of heat or electricity.

CHEMICAL PROPERTIES OF SULFUR

Elements have chemical properties as well as physical properties. Chemical properties are harder to observe. They affect how an element reacts with other substances.

CHEMICAL CHANGES

When one element combines with another, their individual atoms are reordered into new arrangement. This is called a chemical change. An element's chemical properties can be observed during a chemical change. These include how readily it forms bonds, and how easily it burns.

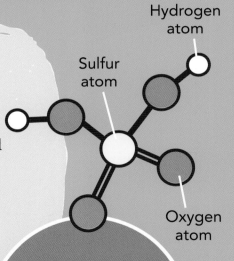

Hydrogen atom

Sulfur atom

Oxygen atom

A molecule of sulfuric acid has one sulfur atom, two hydrogen atoms, and four oxygen atoms.

Where's the Sulfur?

One of sulfur's chemical properties is that it forms compounds easily. Many of these compounds are found in food and cleaning products. Their names often contain "sulf-" or "thio-."

At the Kawah Ijen volcano in Indonesia, sulfuric gases burn to create dazzling blue flames.

ALL ABOUT SULFUR

Studying sulfur's many compounds has helped scientists learn a lot about its chemical properties. Here are a few of them:

Sulfur burns easily, giving off a clear blue flame and a strong odor.

Sulfur can combine with nearly all other elements. It will combine with some at room temperature, but with some others it has to be heated.

Compounds of sulfur and a metal are called sulfides.

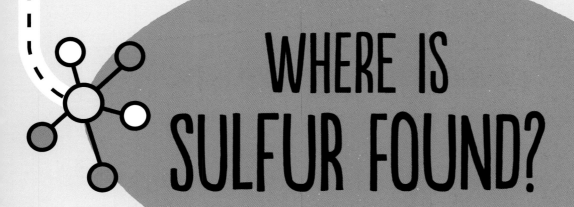

WHERE IS SULFUR FOUND?

Sulfur makes up less than one-tenth of one percent of Earth's crust. However, it is also found in the oceans, and in all living things.

The bodies of all living things include many different sulfur compounds.

Some rocks and minerals are made up of sulfur compounds.

Sulfur compounds called sulfates are found in seawater!

Coal, oil, and natural gas formed from the remains of living things from millions of years ago. They contain sulfur compounds.

Gypsum is a form of a compound called calcium sulfate. There are large underground deposits of gypsum. It was left behind when ancient seas evaporated.

Iron pyrite is a compound formed from iron and sulfur. It is shiny and gold in color. It is often called "fool's gold" because its appearance fooled many gold prospectors hoping to strike it rich.

HOW SULFUR WAS DISCOVERED

HOW SULFUR WAS DISCOVERED

Ancient people knew about sulfur, and it was mentioned in the Bible. Sulfur was used as a pigment, a medicine, and a bleach. By about 500 BC it was being used in explosives and fireworks. French chemist Antoine Lavoisier recognized it as an element in 1777.

Pure sulfur is often found near volcanoes. It collects as crystals near vents where volcanic gases emerge.

SULFUR IN THE BODY

The human body is made up of tiny cells, and each cell is made up of even tinier atoms and molecules. Many of these molecules contain sulfur.

THE BIG FOUR

About 96 percent of the human body is made up of just four elements: oxygen, carbon, hydrogen, and nitrogen. Sulfur is in eighth place, making up less than 1 percent of your body's mass. But although the amount is small, it plays an important role.

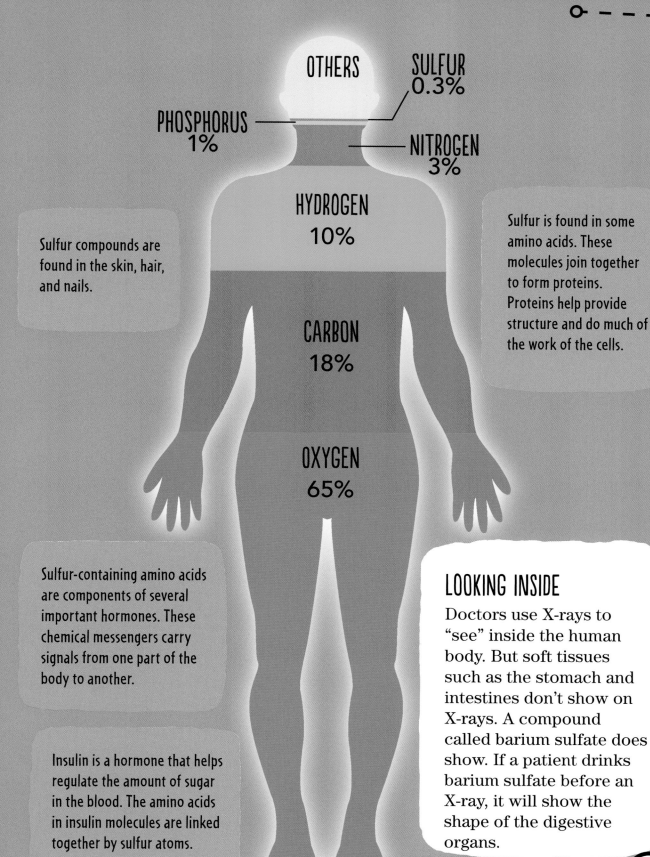

OTHERS

SULFUR
0.3%

PHOSPHORUS
1%

NITROGEN
3%

HYDROGEN
10%

CARBON
18%

OXYGEN
65%

Sulfur compounds are found in the skin, hair, and nails.

Sulfur is found in some amino acids. These molecules join together to form proteins. Proteins help provide structure and do much of the work of the cells.

Sulfur-containing amino acids are components of several important hormones. These chemical messengers carry signals from one part of the body to another.

Insulin is a hormone that helps regulate the amount of sugar in the blood. The amino acids in insulin molecules are linked together by sulfur atoms.

LOOKING INSIDE

Doctors use X-rays to "see" inside the human body. But soft tissues such as the stomach and intestines don't show on X-rays. A compound called barium sulfate does show. If a patient drinks barium sulfate before an X-ray, it will show the shape of the digestive organs.

SULFUR AND LIFE

When it comes to elements that are essential to life, you might think about the oxygen we breathe. Sulfur may be less well known, but it is just as important!

SULFUR AND PLANTS

There is sulfur in the soil, which comes from minerals and from decaying plant and animal matter. Plants take up sulfur through their roots and change it into different compounds. Plants use the sulfur compounds to form proteins and substances called enzymes. Enzymes help speed up the rate of chemical reactions.

The sulfur compounds in plants are essential for the human body.

EATING SULFUR

All animals, including humans, rely on plants for food. They either eat them directly, or they eat plant-eating animals. When animals eat plants, they take in some of this sulfur.

UNDER THE SEA

At the bottom of the ocean, hot water spews out of hydrothermal vents. These places are home to bacteria that get their energy from sulfur compounds in the water. The bacteria release compounds that can be used as food by other organisms.

The tube worms that live on hydrothermal vents rely on the sulfur-processing bacteria.

SULFUR AND MEDICINE

People have used sulfur since ancient times. One of its most important uses was helping to keep people healthy.

People still use many of the hot springs that were popular with ancient people.

ONCE UPON A TIME...

People such as the ancient Romans used to burn sulfur and sulfur compounds, hoping that their strong smell would drive away evil spirits. They also knew that burning sulfur would get rid of mice, ticks, lice, and other pests. Some people took sulfur powder as a medicine, to get rid of intestinal worms.

Some natural hot springs contain sulfur compounds dissolved in the water. For centuries, people have soaked in these hot springs to improve their health.

MODERN MEDICINE

In the 1930s, scientists discovered that a particular type of sulfur compound could kill bacteria. In World War II, soldiers sprinkled sulfur powder on wounds to prevent infection.

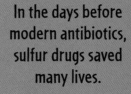

In the days before modern antibiotics, sulfur drugs saved many lives.

That's a Relief!

The compound magnesium sulfate is better known as Epsom salt. People soak in it to soothe sore muscles and sunburned skin, or drink it to improve digestion.

SMELLY SULFUR

Although sulfur has many uses, it is probably most famous for one particular property—its smell!

HYDROGEN SULFIDE

In small amounts, a gas called hydrogen sulfide gives rotten eggs and farts their distinctive smell. In large amounts, it can be deadly. It often forms in swamps and sewers, when plant and animal matter is broken down. Hydrogen sulfide also occurs naturally in volcanic gases and natural gas.

A molecule of hydrogen sulfide has one sulfur atom joined to two hydrogen atoms.

Hydrogen atoms

Sulfur atom

BRIMSTONE

The Bible sometimes refers to a substance called "brimstone." This is just another name for sulfur. People associated its smell with the fires of hell.

THE FLAVOR OF SULFUR

Onions and garlic get their sharp odor and flavor from sulfur compounds. These compounds act as a defense against animals who want to eat the plants. They can make your eyes sting.

Sulfur compounds are also responsible for the pungent taste of mustard and horseradish.

THIOLS

Thiols are another type of sulfur compound with a bad smell. They are found in the stinky liquid that skunks spray. But thiols can be useful! Natural gas doesn't have its own smell. Engineers add a thiol to natural gas so that people can easily sniff out a dangerous leak.

SULFURIC ACID

One of the most important sulfur compounds is a liquid called sulfuric acid. It is dangerous to touch, but it has many uses.

PROPERTIES

Sulfuric acid is a thick, oily, colorless liquid that dissolves easily in water. It is very corrosive, meaning that it will eat away at many substances. Each molecule has one sulfur atom, two hydrogen atoms, and four oxygen atoms, giving it a chemical formula of H_2SO_4. It is sometimes called "oil of vitriol."

Sulfuric acid can cause severe burns, so safety gear is essential when using it.

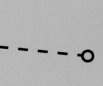

THE KING OF CHEMICALS

Sulfuric acid is so important that some people call it the "king of chemicals." The United States is the world's leading producer, manufacturing 86 billion pounds (39 billion kilograms) every year.

PRODUCTION AND USE

Sulfuric acid can occur in nature, but it is also manufactured in huge quantities. Sulfur is burned to produce sulfur dioxide, then converted to sulfur trioxide. Adding water makes sulfuric acid.

The finished product is incredibly useful. Huge quantities of it are used in the production of fertilizers. It is also used in the refining of crude oil and the manufacture of other chemicals.

There is sulfuric acid in car batteries and drain cleaner.

ACID RAIN

Although sulfuric acid is useful, it can harm the environment. When it falls from the sky in the form of acid rain, it harms living things.

ACID FROM THE SKY

Pure water is neutral—neither an acid nor a base. But most rainwater is actually acidic. It absorbs compounds from the atmosphere, which produce acid when they react with water. A gas galled sulfur dioxide mixes with water to produce sulfuric acid.

This acid is diluted, but it can still cause damage when it falls to Earth. It gets into lakes and rivers, harming the plants and animals that live there. It gets into the soil.

Acid rain eats away at buildings and sculptures made of marble or limestone.

WHERE DOES IT COME FROM?

Some of the sulfur in the atmosphere comes from natural sources, such as volcanoes. But humans are the main source. When we burn fossil fuels such as coal, oil, and natural gas, it releases sulfur dioxide.

Acid rain damages trees and robs the soil of nutrients.

A WORLDWIDE PROBLEM

Because wind blows clouds and weather systems from one place to another, acid rain can cross country borders and fall anywhere. It may fall hundreds of miles away from where the sulfur dioxide was produced.

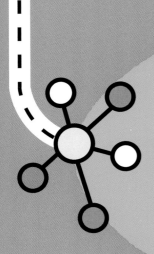

USING SULFUR

Sulfur is essential for life, but it is useful in other ways, too. There is sulfur in many everyday products, and it is used in the manufacture of others.

Sulfur is a key ingredient of gunpowder, which was invented in China more than 1,000 years ago. It is used in guns and in fireworks.

The main use of sulfur is to make fertilizers, which are used on crops around the world. They help farmers grow bigger and better crops.

Sulfur compounds play a role in converting wood into wood pulp for making paper.

Sulfur is used to harden rubber. The process is called vulcanization. It makes the rubber more durable. Tires are made from vulcanized rubber.

Many gardeners use sulfur as a fungicide to protect their plants from fungal diseases.

During World War I, armies used a sulfur compound called mustard gas against enemy troops. It caused severe blisters and burns when it was inhaled or came into contact with the skin.

There are sulfur compounds in many laundry detergents.

THE PERIODIC TABLE

All the elements are organized into a chart called the periodic table. It groups together elements with similar properties. Each square gives information about a particular element.

A Good Idea!

The periodic table was developed in the 1860s by a Russian chemist named Dmitri Mendeleev. He left gaps that were later filled in with new elements, as they were discovered.

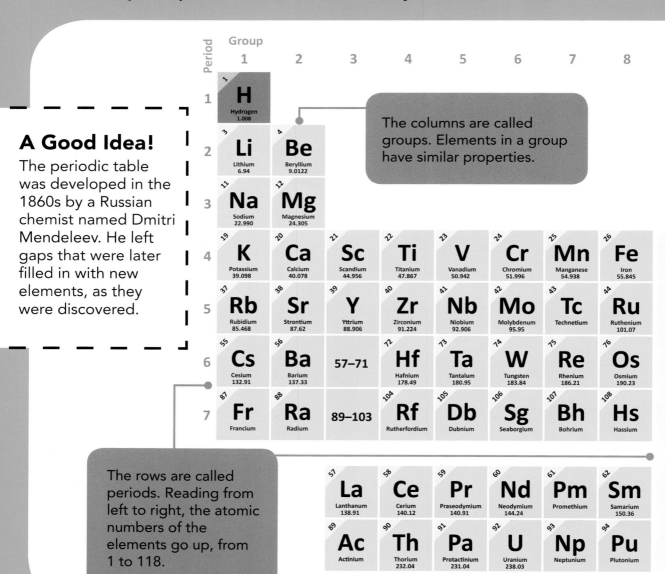

The columns are called groups. Elements in a group have similar properties.

The rows are called periods. Reading from left to right, the atomic numbers of the elements go up, from 1 to 118.

Every element has an atomic number. It shows how many protons are in each of its atoms. Sulfur's atomic number is 16.

The chemical symbol is one or two letters, often an abbreviation of the element's name. It is the same in all languages.

Each square shows the element's name. Different languages use different names.

A number shows the element's atomic weight. It is an average of the number of protons and neutrons in the different isotopes of an element.

16

S
Sulfur
32.06

9	10	11	12	13	14	15	16	17	18

Metalloids (semimetals)

Non–metals

Metals

2
He
Helium
4.0026

5
B
Boron
10.81

6
C
Carbon
12.011

7
N
Nitrogen
14.007

8
O
Oxygen
15.999

9
F
Fluorine
18.998

10
Ne
Neon
20.180

13
Al
Aluminum
26.982

14
Si
Silicon
28.085

15
P
Phosphorus
30.974

16
S
Sulfur
32.06

17
Cl
Chlorine
35.45

18
Ar
Argon
39.948

27 **Co** Cobalt 58.933 | **28** **Ni** Nickel 58.693 | **29** **Cu** Copper 63.546 | **30** **Zn** Zinc 65.38 | **31** **Ga** Gallium 69.723 | **32** **Ge** Germanium 72.630 | **33** **As** Arsenic 74.922 | **34** **Se** Selenium 78.971 | **35** **Br** Bromine 79.904 | **36** **Kr** Krypton 83.798

45 **Rh** Rhodium 102.91 | **46** **Pd** Palladium 106.42 | **47** **Ag** Silver 107.87 | **48** **Cd** Cadmium 112.41 | **49** **In** Indium 114.82 | **50** **Sn** Tin 118.71 | **51** **Sb** Antimony 121.76 | **52** **Te** Tellurium 127.60 | **53** **I** Iodine 126.90 | **54** **Xe** Xenon 131.29

77 **Ir** Iridium 192.22 | **78** **Pt** Platinum 195.08 | **79** **Au** Gold 196.97 | **80** **Hg** Mercury 200.59 | **81** **Tl** Thallium 204.38 | **82** **Pb** Lead 207.2 | **83** **Bi** Bismuth 208.98 | **84** **Po** Polonium | **85** **At** Astatine | **86** **Rn** Radon

109 **Mt** Meitnerium | **110** **Ds** Darmstadtium | **111** **Rg** Roentgenium | **112** **Cn** Copernicium | **113** **Nh** Nihonium | **114** **Fl** Flerovium | **115** **Mc** Moscovium | **116** **Lv** Livermorium | **117** **Ts** Tennessine | **118** **Og** Oganesson

63 **Eu** Europium 151.96 | **64** **Gd** Gadolinium 157.25 | **65** **Tb** Terbium 158.93 | **66** **Dy** Dysprosium 162.50 | **67** **Ho** Holmium 164.93 | **68** **Er** Erbium 167.26 | **69** **Tm** Thulium 168.93 | **70** **Yb** Ytterbium 173.05 | **71** **Lu** Lutetium 174.97

Lanthanide elements

95 **Am** Americium | **96** **Cm** Curium | **97** **Bk** Berkelium | **98** **Cf** Californium | **99** **Es** Einsteinium | **100** **Fm** Fermium | **101** **Md** Mendelevium | **102** **No** Nobelium | **103** **Lr** Lawrencium

Actinide elements

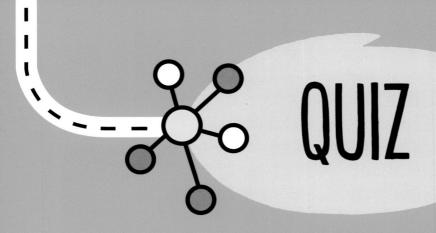

QUIZ

Try this quiz and test your knowledge of sulfur and elements! The answers are on page 32.

1

What are electrons?

a. the times when you vote for politicians

b. tiny particles that are found in atoms

c. the beats in a dance music track

2

What does hydrogen sulfide smell like?

a. chocolate

b. rotten eggs

c. coffee

3

What can happen when pure sulfur melts?

a. it gets really stringy, just like mozzarella

b. it turns into acid rain

c. it changes from yellow to reddish-brown

4

What nickname is often given to iron pyrite?

a. fool's gold

b. idiot's silver

c. clown's copper

5

Why do doctors ask patients to drink barium sulfate?

a. to see if their sense of taste is working

b. to kill germs inside their body

c. to make their organs show up on X-rays

6

Why did soldiers sprinkle sulfur powder on wounds?

a. it helped prevent infection

b. it soaked up some of the blood

c. they thought it would drive away evil spirits

7

Why do engineers add a sulfur compound to natural gas?

a. to make it burn more cleanly

b. so that people can easily smell a gas leak

c. so that energy companies can charge more for it

8

What happens when you add sulfur to natural rubber?

a. it starts to smell like farts

b. it turns into sulfuric acid

c. the rubber becomes harder and more durable

GLOSSARY

acid a substance with a low pH that has a sour taste and eats away other materials

allotropes different forms of the same element. Allotropes of an element have the atoms arranged in different patterns.

amino acid substance that is necessary for building proteins

atmosphere the layers of gases that surround the earth

atom the smallest possible unit of a chemical element

bacteria tiny living things that can cause infection but that can also be useful, such as by breaking down dead matter

base a substance with a high pH; the opposite of an acid

bond to form a link with other atoms of the same element or of a different element

cell the smallest unit of life. All plants and animals are made of cells.

chemical change change that occurs when one substance reacts with another to form a new substance

chemical property characteristic of a material that can be observed during or after a chemical reaction

compound substance made of two or more different elements bonded together

conductor substance that allows heat or electricity to pass through it easily

crust the hard, outermost layer of Earth

durable long-lasting and able to stand wear and tear

electron a tiny particle of an atom. Electrons have a negative charge

element a substance that cannot be broken down or separated into other substances

energy the ability to do work. Energy can take many different forms.

evaporate to turn from a liquid into a gas

fossil fuels fuels such as oil, coal, and natural gas that are formed from the decaying remains of living things

gas form of matter that is neither liquid or solid

hormone substance in the body that can carry chemical messages

isotopes different forms of the same element. Isotopes of an element have different numbers of neutrons.

liquid form of matter that is neither a solid nor a gas, and flows when it is poured

mass the total amount of matter in an object or space

molecule the smallest unit of a substance that has all the properties of that substance. A molecule can be made up of a single atom, or a group of atoms

natural gas mixture of methane and other gases that is often burned as a fuel

neutron a particle in the nucleus of an atom with no electrical charge

oxygen gas found in the air that living things need in order to survive

physical property characteristic of a material that can be observed without changing the material

proton a positively charged particle in the nucleus of an atom

react to undergo a chemical change when combined with another substance

FURTHER RESOURCES

BOOKS

Arbuthnott, Gill. *Your Guide to the Periodic Table.* New York, NY: Crabtree Publishing Company, 2016.

Callery, Sean, and Miranda Smith. *Periodic Table.* New York, NY: Scholastic Nonfiction, 2017.

Orr, Tamra B. *Antibiotics.* New York, NY: Scholastic, 2017.

Sawyer, Ava. *Humans and Earth's Atmosphere: What's in the Air?* North Mankato, MN: Capstone Press, 2018.

WEBSITES

Find out more about sulfur:
www.ducksters.com/science/chemistry/sulfur.php

This Environmental Protection Agency has more information about acid rain:
www.epa.gov/acidrain/what-acid-rain

Go here for amazing facts about sulfur:
www.livescience.com/28939-sulfur.html

Learn about all the elements using this interactive periodic table:
www.rsc.org/periodic-table/

INDEX

acid rain 22, 23
acids 20–21, 22, 23
allotropes 6, 7
amino acids 13
artificial elements 5
atomic numbers and weights
    26, 27
atoms 4, 5, 6, 8, 12, 13, 18, 20, 27

bacteria 15, 17
barium sulfate 13
bonds 8
brimstone 18
burning 8, 9

carbon 4, 12
cells 12, 13
chemical changes 8
chemical formulas 20
chemical properties 8–9
chemical reactions 14
color 7
compounds 5, 7, 8, 9, 10, 11, 13,
    14, 15, 19, 20, 25
conductivity 7
crystals 7

discovery of sulfur 11

electrons 4
elements 4, 5, 26–27
enzymes 14

fertilizers 21, 25
foods 14, 15, 19
fossil fuels 10, 23

gunpowder 24
gypsum 10

hardness 7
hormones 13
hot springs 16
human body, sulfur in the 12–13
hydrogen 4, 8, 12, 18, 20
hydrogen sulfide 18
hydrothermal vents 15

insulin 13
iron pyrite ("fool's gold") 11
isotopes 27

magnesium sulfate (Epsom salt)
    17
medicinal uses 16–17
molecules 8, 12, 13, 18, 20
mustard gas 25

natural elements 5
neutrons 4, 27
nitrogen 4, 12

odor 7, 9, 16, 18–19
oxygen 4, 8, 12, 20

periodic table 26–27
phosphorus 4
physical properties 6–7
plants 14, 25
proteins 13, 14
protons 4, 27

rocks and minerals 5, 10, 14

sources of sulfur 5, 10–11, 23
sulfates 10
sulfides 9
sulfur dioxide 22, 23
sulfuric acid 20–21, 22

thiols 19

uses for sulfur 16–17, 21, 24–25

volcanoes 5, 9, 11, 18, 23
vulcanization 25

X-rays 13

Quiz answers
1. b; 2. b; 3. c; 4. a; 5. c;
6. a; 7. b; 8. c